YOU RUINED ME, MY LOVE

A BOOK OF HER LINES

PRAVALLIKA SAI

"You Ruined Me, My Love" is dedicated to readers who find themselves alone when they fall in love.

That pain, as well as your love for the special one, remains within you.
to find out why!

Why does it always have to be me?

Why am I behaving like a love victim when I am my life's main character?

Why am I a bystander in the life of someone I used to love?

Why Me? Why?

Imagine yourself as "he" from the word "she" and "him" from the word "her" if you are a male reading this book.

The lines in this book that I wrote may provide you with an answer.

Contents

Contents

Contents

Contents

Contents

Preface

Greetings to the readers!

This is about the type of love that will leave you in tears by the end. Some call it "unrequited love," while others call it "one-sided love."

Whatever name they give it, the result is emptiness and pain to force us to change and learn the lesson without cheating for the sake of our future.

There is no success without pain. Whether it's about love, a career, or anything, it makes no difference. Pain makes people stronger.

Those who have been through pain can reap rewards such as a happy life!

Remember that when no one loves you, you are in the present moment, not in the future.

1. Sad Tune

"When I see you,

My soul sang a wonderful love song.

Until you dedicate your love song to someone

Now,

My wonderful love song becomes sad."

- Pravallika Sai

2. Fueling Our Feelings

"Unrequited love is analogous to
Fueling our emotions with the incorrect fuel
In the end,
We must turn off our emotions.
and keep our hearts safe.
Otherwise, it will be lost forever.
Our hearts will be damaged."

- Pravallika Sai

3. Fading Flower

"How can you grow?
That never-fading flower
as if you were smiling
with your tears every day."

- Pravallika Sai

4. Express Feelings

*"She did not know.
how to express her feelings.
That's why she ended up
being involved in an "unanswered love""*

- Pravallika Sai

5. Smells Like Love

"She smells like love.
But he did not sense it.
Perhaps he has anosmia."

- Pravallika Sai

6. Mother Earth

"They say women have
The patience of mother earth
But that patience will die.
when she wasn't treated right."

- Pravallika Sai

7. Elixir

"*To meet love is a sin*
To believe in love is an elixir
Is one type of curse."

- Pravallika Sai

8. Bleed

"She enjoys reading.
She adores writing.
She muses
Why we cannot "bleed" from words"

- Pravallika Sai

9. Melted

"*She melted in his presence.*
Like
In the light, a candle melts."

- Pravallika Sai

10. Unreciprocated Love

11. Heart Disease

"If she goes for a walk in the rain,

She gets cold.

If she was with the boisterous crowd,

She gets a headache.

If she is close to the dust,

She is allergic to dust.

She will be healthier if she spends more time outside in the

sun.

She falls as a result of a vitamin deficiency.

But,

If she was near you or with you,

She develops "heart disease."

- Pravallika Sai

12. Prayer Chant

13. Someone

"If there is no love,

Nobody loves anyone.

When there is love,

One is loved by Someone else.

But

That, someone, was never me"

\- *Pravallika Sai*

14. Dear Mother

"Dear Mother,
You said that what we give
It will always come back to us.
I gave love
But nothing came back.
Why mom? Why?"

- Pravallika Sai

15. Dance

"She enjoys dancing.
So she danced in the rain, remembering him.
Until she noticed
He was dancing in the rain with someone."

- Pravallika Sai

16. Magic

"She is pure enchantment.
He despised magic.
Perhaps he is the sceptical type."

- Pravallika Sai

17. Chutki

"*She is a chutki.*
He is a Chota Bheem.
But
He chose Indumati.
which left the fans "heartbroken.""

- Pravallika Sai

18. Gun

"*Unrequited love is analogous to*
Give a gun to someone you care about.
and instruct them to shoot
to find out if he loved her or not
However, he shot her.
Until the gun was empty of bullets,
and then threw the gun at her
He walked away without even thinking he'd made a
mistake."

- Pravallika Sai

19. Books

> "*Unrequited love is similar to*
> *She cannot give her love to another person.*
> *Therefore, she decided to compose*
> *Adding her love to the written word*
> *It might not be able to survive elsewhere.*"
>
> *- Pravallika Sai*

20. Drama

"She despises drama.
If there is so much drama surrounding her,
She will leave when the opportunity to act presents itself.
But she had no idea.
In the drama, the one she loves was a fantastic actor."

- Pravallika Sai

21. One-Sided Love

"Unrequited love is a type of love
that is also referred to as"
One-sided Love

22. She

"*She is sad.*
She is unhappy.
She is sorrowful.
She is dejected.
She is upset.
She is heartbroken.
She is cheerless.
She is painful.
She is joyless.
She is heartbroken.
She is hurting.
She is tearful.
She is disappointed.
She is heavy-hearted.
However, now
She was determined to combat anything that made her
unhappy."

- Pravallika Sai

23. Ruined

*"Even though
He destroyed her.
She did not destroy him.
Because she isn't "him."*

- Pravallika Sai

24. No One Waits

"She sat there and waited for him.
But
He didn't bother waiting for her.
Because
She has no idea.
"No One Waits" in this generation."

- Pravallika Sai

25. Lesson

"Lessons at school or college

The teacher can take it.

But

She eventually

Taking a valuable lesson from him,

Her heart must be taught."

- Pravallika Sai

26. Change

"She had thought
Each year, only the seasons may be modified.
However, she realized
People will also change."

- Pravallika Sai

27. Princess

"She truly is a princess.
But
He is not a crown prince.
This is why
He left the palace."

- Pravallika Sai

28. Tax

"She gave him her complete attention.
But
Obtaining a 20% return
Did she strike him as a tax?"

- Pravallika Sai

29. Scared

"She becomes terrified.

When

Someone will fall in love with her one day.

And

The next day, they decide they don't want her."

- Pravallika Sai

30. Water

"You find it impossible to maintain
Pouring water from the bottom of your heart
Something that isn't even required
A single drop of water
It's a waste of both water and energy."

- Pravallika Sai

31. Unreturned Love

"Unrequited love is a type of love
that is also referred to as"
Unreturned Love

32. Shut Down

"She figured out how to turn her emotions off.
So,
Nothing can hurt her anymore."

- Pravallika Sai

33. Toxic

"Toxic people are dangerous.
Toxic people are unhealthy.
Toxic people are unsafe.
Toxic people are terrible.
Toxic people are precarious.
Toxic people are hazardous.
Because
You will adore them wholeheartedly.
without even noticing
Your heart is aching.
As a result of them"

- Pravallika Sai

34. Eiffel Tower

"She pondered.
An Eiffel Tower, he was.
but eventually learned
He is a tower for cell phones."

- Pravallika Sai

35. Eraser

"Unrequited love is similar to
Using a pencil to write a story
unaware of that
When the eraser enters, the story will vanish."

- Pravallika Sai

36. Pain

*"She can't bear the thought of her dog being sad.
However, she ended up in pain.
By adoring him
rather than him
The dog consulted her."*

- Pravallika Sai

37. Thorns

"*She is a lovely rose.*
She wished for thorns.
That is how she met him.
And
She had enough thorns"

- Pravallika Sai

38. Lifebuoy

*"Lifebuoy's specialization is to give both protection and care.
Where,
His specialty is making her deal with both pain and trust concerns."*

- Pravallika Sai

39. Crushed

"He was her crush, she thought.
As a result, he crushed her.
She now understands what it's like to be crushed by her
crush."

- Pravallika Sai

40. Skeleton

"Unrequited love is similar to a skeleton.
It will be beautiful.
When it is given skin by someone else"

- Pravallika Sai

41. Unanswered Love

"*Unrequited love is a type of love
that is also referred to as*"
Unanswered Love

42. Answer

"She finally got it.
why he left without saying anything
She discovered that
"No answer is also an answer."

- Pravallika Sai

43. Sometimes

"She disliked the phrase "sometimes."

Because

She doesn't want to be someone else's sometimes."

- Pravallika Sai

44. Fool

"She despised his little games.
She didn't like his acting abilities.
Because
He forced her to play the fool.
But
He was completely unaware. She was not a fool.
What could be worse?
Falling in love with a fool
Or
Making a fool of yourself by falling in love
Oh, I adore you.
People are duped by love."

- Pravallika Sai

45. Song

"She is a song of forever.
But
He did not even play it."

- Pravallika Sai

46. Touch-Me-Not

"Love that goes unrequited is like a touch-me-not plant.
when we begin to experience love
Once love is gone, it crumbles.
till the heart stops entirely"

- Pravallika Sai

47. Not Mine

"The eyes are mine
the tears coming from the eyes are also mine
the hands that weep my tears are also mine
but you are not mine"

- Pravallika Sai

48. Eyes

"Up until yesterday,
Your presence filled my eyes.
And now,
My eyes are questioning and arguing with me.
Where is my love?
So she responded to her gaze.
I have no regrets; he is gone for good."

- Pravallika Sai

49. Zombie

"Just like a zombie,
The dreaded "walking dead"
Unrequited love creates
Human Zombie Forms
Like
The Walking Dead"

- Pravallika Sai

50. Glasses

> *"She already has a limited vision of the outside world.*
> *Without her glasses*
> *But,*
> *She expected to be able to see his heart through her glasses.*
> *What a fool she was."*
>
> *- Pravallika Sai*

51. Ruin

"Similar to how a father might sabotage his child's life,
Particularly when the child needs the father the most and
he is not there.
similar to what the child's father did,
You treated me in the same manner.
And you, my love, have ruined my life!"

- Pravallika Sai

52. Unhealthy

"Junk food is bad for you.
which influences our health
Unrequited love is harmful.
which harms our hearts"

- Pravallika Sai

53. Shortest Time

"Consider the time you have with him to be a gift from the gods.

And

Avoid the debt of love that did not happen."

- Pravallika Sai

54. Values

"To construct a home,
There is a demand for materials such as sand, bricks, steel,
concrete, glass, and plastic.
To foster love,
It is necessary to uphold values like respect, comprehension,
sharing, responsibility, etc."

- Pravallika Sai

55. Traffic Lights

"*Unrequited love is*
like traffic lights
Where
The red colour indicates there is no love.
The green colour indicates that maybe there is a chance.
The yellow colour indicates that you never know.
When you are going to move
Until you receive a green signal"

- Pravallika Sai

56. Realization

"She was convinced.
Her life will be better now that she has him.
However, in the end,
She realized her life was better without him.
There is no pain, no lack of trust, nothing...
It was a lovely life in which she discovered true
happiness."

- Pravallika Sai

57. Ever

"She had feelings for him.

But

He had no feelings for her.

Did he ever look back and reflect?

Oh god! She loved me so much, and I yearned for her."

- Pravallika Sai

58. God

"*She prayed to the deity for a sign.*
if he is the right person,
Dark thunder, heavy rain, and violent storms were used by
God as a form of retort.
The response from God alarmed her.
She realized at this point that "he is not the one.""

- Pravallika Sai

59. Cursed

"*She has been cursed.*

to be forgotten by everyone she comes into contact with

And

She was certain he would never forget her.

But

He eventually left her without even looking back."

- Pravallika Sai

60. Mess

"Unrequited love is harmful.
At first glance, it appears to be a lovely sensation.
Until he changes his mind
Pose a question to yourself.
How did I get myself into this situation?"

- Pravallika Sai

61. Rejected Love

"Unrequited love is a type of love that is also referred to as Rejected Love"

62. About Her

"One feature she admired in herself was
Regardless of how she has been treated,
Regardless of what she is going through
Regardless of how she feels
She still has a diamond heart.
an infinite abundance of love to give
That is something no one can ever take away from her."

- *Pravallika Sai*

63. Why Me?

"*A part of her will always is curious.*
Why does it always have to be just me?
Why, why, why, God?
Why did it never happen to anyone else?
Why did the pain pick me?
Why Me?
This pain kills me."

- Pravallika Sai

64. Beautiful

"Even if you didn't notice, she's beautiful.
She wished for what every young heart wishes for.
For something beautiful to find her beautiful"

- Pravallika Sai

65. Discovered

"They claim that loving you is a losing game.

He believes she was defeated in the game.

But

She had never been defeated.

She was victorious.

She Discovers

She took a stand for herself.

She is forgiving.

She develops

She gains strength.

Last but not least

She discovered herself"

- Pravallika Sai

66. Seetha

"She is Seetha.
He was her Rama, she thought.
but eventually discovered
He resembles Krishna but not Rama."

- Pravallika Sai

67. Hurt

"*You may live your life in whatever you wish.*
But that doesn't mean you can have fun.
By damaging the feelings of others toward you"

- Pravallika Sai

68. Main Character

"She is the main character.
But he has given her a side-character role.
Hence, she left the chapter."

- Pravallika Sai

69. Sky

"*She is the sky.*
He represents the cloud.
The sky remains unchanged, but
The clouds will clear.
because clouds do not float forever"

- Pravallika Sai

70. Special

"She thought he was unique in some way.
When her imagination had run wild
He was similar to the rest of us, she realized.
Nothing unusual about having two hands, two legs, a face,
eyes, nose, mouth, and ears as a human being but with a
heart where she cannot enter."

- Pravallika Sai

71. Bigoted Love

72. Tulasi

"She is a Tulasi plant
it was beneficial to the health
But he likes fancy flowers. "

- Pravallika Sai

73. Life

"If you are with me,
If you are not with me,
What does it make a difference?
I always ended up adoring you by myself.
Life was unforgiving.
and is ruthless..."

- Pravallika Sai

74. Love Story

"*Some individuals write love stories in a book using a pen.*
Some individuals use a gadget to create love stories while
typing words on a keyboard.
Some people create fantasy worlds in which they write love
stories.
But,
I'm working on my love tale.
Tears as a Pencil
To me, my eyes are like a book.
My hands are like erasers, erasing the tears.
with a gloomy expression on my face
In my eyes, I can see the love and pain."

- Pravallika Sai

75. You Don't Know

"How can I express my feelings for you?

Oh, dear.

I can't tell you.

In my eyes, you can see my heart's thoughts.

It will be explained to you through the eyes.

Have you heard?

Did you get the point?

Do you realize how much I care about you?

If you have heard

If you comprehend

If you know how I feel, you'll understand

So, my darling, why did you abandon me?

You have no idea how much I adore you; I haven't even

shown it to you.

I thought my eyes could express how much you meant to

me.

You have no idea, my darling.

You have no idea"

- Pravallika Sai

76. Pain

"Pain is unbearable.
Pain is insufferable.
Pain is unendurable.
Pain is agonizing.
Pain is racking
The pain is heavy.
Pain is torture
Pain is discomfort.
Pain is trouble.
The pain is getting worse.
Last but not least
The Pain Is You"

- Pravallika Sai

77. It's Okay

"She had feelings for him.

He had feelings for someone.

It's fine. It's not always our day.

It's fine. It's not always our day.

It's Okay to Cry.

It is OK to be injured.

It's All Right to Love Someone Who Doesn't Return Your

Love

It's OK to not be okay."

- Pravallika Sai

78. Let Go

"She had feelings for him.
He has feelings for someone.
She realized what he was doing to her.
She can now let go much more easily."

- Pravallika Sai

79. Wound

"Every recollection of my love is hurt.
Every wound has turned into a goal.
These goals have become landmarks in my love life."

- Pravallika Sai

80. Fire

"*Memories of the Past*

I spent some time with you.

as though there was a secret fire in my heart

You lit a fire in my heart.

I had permitted you to destroy it.

My heart is now filled with gloom.

Welcome to the darkness."

- Pravallika Sai

81. Unbalanced Love

*"Unrequited love is a type of love
that is also referred to as"*
Unbalanced Love

82. Star

"She fell in love with him.
As a star,
falls from the sky"

- Pravallika Sai

83. Sad

"If I am not available,
There is no sadness.
If I'm not speaking to you,
There is no sadness.
If I am not present to enjoy your joy,
There is no sadness.
If I am unable to see you every day,
There is no sadness.
If I am not present to inquire how you are,
There is no sadness.
If I am not present to check on you,
There is no sadness.
Even if my presence is unimportant to you
Please don't be sad."

-Pravallika Sai

84. She Knows

"*She's positive she'll fall in love.*
This is due to
She is also a human being.
How about she?
She has been waiting for you for a long time.
Was all of that unimportant to you?
He departed, and she had no idea that was his last
farewell.
She has decided to keep him as her favorite. Unfulfilled
Wish"

- Pravallika Sai

85. Movies

"She fantasized about the type of love she saw in movies.

But

She was cast in a sad love tale movie."

- Pravallika Sai

86. Never Again

"He never followed through on his words.
However, I'm glad I lived there.
Thank you for your time.
But I'll never fall in love again."

- Pravallika Sai

87. Difficult

"And finally,
Regardless of how hard I try
It's tough to quit loving you."

- Pravallika Sai

88. Done

"*I'm tired of feeling unworthy.*
I'm sick of loving hard yet getting little in return.
You hit me where it hurts"

- Pravallika Sai

89. No Longer

*"I made a mistake by falling for you.
We could put all of your lies in the box I discovered.
Only you were aware of my feelings for you.
After one disappointment, another occurs.
But you will never be let down.
However, I no longer adore you."*

- Pravallika Sai

90. Happy

"*She wants to laugh at the spots where she cried the most.*
to change the course of her life
She is now happy."

- Pravallika Sai

91. One-Way Love

*"Unrequited love is a type of love that is also referred to
as"*
Oneway Love

92. Accepted

"She has finally accepted one thing about love.
She'll never be loved as much as she loves herself."

- Pravallika Sai

93. Heartache

"She had feelings for him.
She scribbled a love letter.
however, in exchange
He wrote of her heartache, not love."

- Pravallika Sai

94. Fooled

"You had me tricked from the beginning.
I noticed it from a distance.
However, my eyes were deceiving me."

- Pravallika Sai

95. Hate

"When people change, feelings fade.
secrets, lies, excuses
I remained the same, while you played your games.
We're now left with nothing.
I hate wasting my time."

- Pravallika Sai

96. Heartbreak

"The greatest part about heartbreak is
that it is never permanent.
Maybe in the future,
Someone will come and clear the mess
and show you the real meaning of love."

- Pravallika Sai

97. Story

"Unfinished tales remain unfinished.
People even think it's not a real love story.
Even though some believe it is not a real love tale, nothing
changes for the one who is loved."

- Pravallika Sai

98. Why?

"She was sick of being hurt over and over.
She'll ask you one more time.
So why not me?
Is it painful to be with me?
Why won't you choose me?"

- Pravallika Sai

99. It's Over

"How can you tell when it's over?
Perhaps you are more in love with your memories than
with the person."

- Pravallika Sai

100. Adieu

"*the person who*

left me

I appreciate the lesson.
Adieu"

- Pravallika Sai

101. Undeserved Love

> *"Unrequited love is a type of love that is also referred to as"*
>
> *Undeserved Love*

102. 2022

"*To 2022*
Thank you very much.
I matured and got through it."

- Pravallika Sai

103. Depart

"the main focus is
the way they leave you
because it represents
how loyal they were to you"

- Pravallika Sai

104. Changed

*"I've altered every element of myself to the point where
where the puzzle pieces no longer represent me"*

- Pravallika Sai

105. Sometimes

"And sometimes
Just you and your feelings exist.
No one has experienced that.
until they face it."

- Pravallika Sai

106. She Used To

*"She used to enjoy it, but not any longer.
She used to believe, but not anymore.
She used to be concerned, but not anymore.
She used to speak, but not any longer.
She no longer smiles as much as she used to."*

- Pravallika Sai

107. New beginning

"When a child first learns to walk, he will fall.
When a student is learning to write, he will make
mistakes.
When a person tries to love, he fails.
Knowing that failure is not the end
It's a new beginning."

- Pravallika Sai

108. Love = Technology

> - *A human is comparable to technological advancements such as artificial intelligence, machine learning, etc.*
> - *Many people will enroll in the course, complete it and pursue a career in it.*

Many individuals will approach a person to make love.

> - *Some students finish the course and get the certification.*

As a result of their communication, some people become friends and form special bonds.

> - *However, only a few people may obtain it because they are passionate about that technology.*

On the other hand, love can only be earned by one person."

- Pravallika Sai

109. Sacrificed

110. Unsatisfied Love

*"Unrequited love is a type of love
that is also referred to as"
Unsatisfied Love*

End

Finally, I finished writing about love that cannot be returned.

I believe that a thousand-mile journey begins with a single step, and this book is that single step.

This book's final page is all about how you might have liked the lines.

The little miss didn't know how to express her emotions, so she poured them into this book.

Some feelings lingered within her, but it was enough for her to give it a shot with her first book.

Remember that this was not the conclusion, but rather the beginning of a new chapter in the future.

Thank you for taking the time to read this, my dear readers.

You can check my Instagram page: __her__writings__

See you in the next book.